NOTICE

A Wesleyan Chapbook

NOTICE

Rae Armantrout

Wesleyan University Press
Middletown, Connecticut

Wesleyan University Press
Middletown, Connecticut 06459
www.weslpress.org

ISBN 978-0-8195-0101-1

CONTENTS

NOTICE

The way a gesture
used to ward off trouble
became cheerful waving.

There was so much looming
and vanishing

to take note of
always;

we felt like play actors

before we knew
what we were about

and after.

*

Turns out
the mummy's curse

is real.

You pump thick death
out of the ground
and burn it –

it kills you.

But in all the movies
curses are a cheap
plot trick.

The doofus
who can't read the hieroglyph
dies first

and no one misses him.

Them.

We were born yesterday.
We're sorry.

ON GROWTH

Dressed all in plastic,
which means oil,

we're bright-eyed, scrambling
for the colored cubes

spilled
on the rug's polymer.

Inside each
is a tiny car.

When we can't unscrew the tops
we cry for help.

We're optimists.

*

To sleep is to fall
into belief.

Airing even
our worst suspicions
may be pleasurable;

we are carried,
buoyed.

In sleep,
the body can heal itself,
grow larger.

Creatures that never wake
can sprout a whole new
limb,

a tail.

This may be wrong.

ARCH

1

Like an arched eyebrow
traveling alone, you drift,

seahorse,

a forgotten, persistent
question.

Despite your skeptical
attitude, it's true

that your numbers are crashing.

Still, you are rumored
to consume

up to 3,000 baby
shrimp per day!

2

Who doesn't want
to be a revenant,

to go back to basics
in a big way

on the small screen
which, somehow, still

survives? "Terrific"
and "terrible"

are cousins after all.
Am I warm or cold?

I'm half-
rhyming, aiming right

between quick and dead
like we could

thread that needle
and keep going.

AUDIENCE

1

Phlegmatic and unbending,

Russell Crowe as Noah

teaches us

to hold the door

against "the desperate"

and "the many"

threatened by catastrophic

climate change—

worse than we'd guessed

and more immediate.

2

Are we stowaways?

3

Zipper fracture

involves simultaneous

stimulation of parallel

horizontal wells.

Viscoelastic

surfactant gel

has/has not been

adequately described

FREEZE TAG

In spring when the firethorn
pimples with hard buds.

In summer when the rose
drops its rosy discards.

In fall when the trees
go up in flames.

In winter when the kitsch
fantasies of shelter
go on sale.

In spring when,
full of toxins, we're interred
in today's clothes.

TOO MUCH INFORMATION

1

Dears,

the backwards-facing S,
a decoration in the iron rail,
was here when I came,
with its extra curlicues
at each end,
and a miniature
version of itself
like a fetus
affixed to its middle.

I'm telling you more, perhaps,
than you need to know.

The sun on the rail's
inner curves
is a private matter,
something like love,
despite the roar

of the nearby freeway.

I mix love up with safety.

   2

It's hard to come by good
ideas
while California
goes up in flames.

It's hard to have
a new idea
when temps in LA
rival those in Iran.

I can't say anything
more original than:
"Gender Reveal Party
Sparks Massive Wildfire"
in tinder-dry forest.

3

You never know
what will matter next.

Pack everything.

RIDDANCE

Ok, we've rendered
the rendition

how often?

What were we trying
to get rid of?

We exposed the homeless
character of desire
to the weather.

Shall we talk
about the weather

worsening four times
faster than expected,

eight times,

until the joy
of pattern recognition

kicks in?

> Until the crest
> of the next ridge
> is what remains
> of division.

SPECULATIVE FICTION

1

The idea that producing a string of
                              nonsense syllables
while pointing toward an object
may cause that object to change
is common in children on the verge of language.

                *

The idea that force exists only
as an interaction between objects
while an object
is a kind of kink
            in a force field.

          *

The idea that, if one survives X number of years,

one will live to see how things "turn out"
or even that things "end well."

    2

In the future we will face new problems.

How will we represent the variety of human types
once all the large animals are gone?

As sly as a mother;
as hungry as an orphan?

PREVIEWS

1

There are worldwide, catastrophic storms
when earth's network
of weather control satellites
is sabotaged by unknown enemies.

As fire rages through the western forest
Jeff Bridges snarls,
"If you want a piece of me,
come get me."

2

The baby says, "Mmm, mmm!"
to the stuffed fish
then hits it
against her closed mouth.

"Ah, ah," she says,
holding it at a distance.

She opens and closes
the palm of one hand. "Bye-bye,"
we say for her.
"Bye-bye, Fishy!"

PREPAREDNESS

Animals find us eerie.
We can see what's coming

in broad strokes—

washed out,
frequently displaced.

Still, it smites us.

Like ghosts we pass back and forth
between times,

stunned,

unable to feel
what we touch.

We believe in abstractions.

    *

That's one way to explain
our failure to prepare.

MY ERASURES

My erasures were featured.

     *

I collected debris
to sell as crash art,

               crush porn.

     *

"Say goodbye to Lonesome George,"
the last Galapagos tortoise.

     *

I was a pushover
for the laws
of physics.

*

I pictured us as two seals
hauled out
on a sunny rock,

the roar around us
a matter of course

PERSONALS

The symbols are inoperative.

    Worry about the expanse
    of dark water

The "done" button
doesn't work.

    The relentless march of cattails
    into northern lakes

    The blanket of cloud
    cover

"Your response needed"

    A plaintive address
    to a phantom
    beloved

*

I'm into nuance, quaver,
half-notes.

I am half-hearted,
forked tongued.

PANICLE

The hope is that the fungal
mycelium
exchange messages
through a vast underground network.

The hope is that
we're not alone.

A small black spider
cautiously explores
the wet plastic trash bag.

A woman somewhere
across the street
says, "I don't know,"
and laughs.

The hope is in the facts.

Buzzing, a bee slams
time and again
against a blue-black wall.

The hope is that the universe
is formed
of an infinite number
of Y shaped prongs,

rocking stiffly in the wind,
spitting out
lilac panicles.

WHITE SKY

I want to end on something hopeful.

Someone has proposed
we seed the stratosphere

with diamond particles
reflecting back the sun.

I want to know
if they'll twinkle.

Obviously, the stars are bad
role models—

distant, self-absorbed, and
volatile.

Explosions count as "standard
candles."

Some say
we will need to change

the animals.

HERE I GO

1

"Here I go again"
was a rock anthem once,
crowds on their feet
mouthing the words.

2

There's no way to explain
how faultlessly I want to write
about how pointless all this is.

Nothing I can point to, but
the gesture itself,
the way it comes to seem
anachronistic, spectral—

like this ongoing attempt
to catalog the world
by latching each thing

to the last
memory it calls up.

Nothing recalls
the new cat-6
haboob.

3

But I'm hard to discourage.

When a branch lays out five—
like an old card trick—
identical white orchids,

three-petalled light sails spread,

ready to go—each with a small
bat face in the middle

Rae Armantrout is the author of fifteen books of poetry including *Partly: New and Selected Poems, 2001—2015* and *Versed*, winner of the Pulitzer Prize for poetry and the National Book Critics Circle Award.

Poems in this chapbook first appeared in the following Wesleyan University Press books.

Wobble (2018): Arch, Audience, My Erasures
Conjure (2020): Notice, Speculative Fiction, Previews
Finalists (2022): On Growth, Too Much Information, Riddance, Panicle
Go Figure (2024): Freeze Tag, Preparedness, Personals, White Sky, Here I go

Wesleyan Chapbooks

Death of the Poets by Kit Reed,
Illustrated by Joseph W. Reed

Dog Truths by Kit Reed,
Illustrated by Joseph W. Reed

Entanglements by Rae Armantrout

*I Will Teach You about Murder: 29 Love
Poems*, edited by Shea Fitzpatrick, Sallie
Fullerton, and Torii Johnson

Thirty Polite Things to Say by Kit Reed,
Illustrated by Joseph W. Reed